In the Secret Place

Conversations With God

Priscar Manei

ISBN: 978-0-9565780-0-6

Published by

Manei Publications

Printed in the United States of America and the United Kingdom

Foreword

Priscar Manei is a woman of prayer. She has also begun writing some great books. I believe she inherited part of my prophetic mantle from serving very diligently and faithfully in our European office. The words and messages in this book are supernatural and life-enhancing. Enjoy and look for more great works from her in future days.

Dr. Thomas Manton IV
Founder/CEO Dominion International
www.ThomasManton.com

This book is packed with spiritual encouragement for the Christian who wants to grow closer to the invisible God, the compassionate one who revealed himself in Jesus. No one said it would be easy to develop intimate friendship with this God, but the author reveals that if one is willing to take the time and make the commitment, one can know the God of the universe.

Steve Fortosis
author of *The Anchor: Finding Safety in God's Harbour*

I highly recommend that every Christian seeking to find more intimacy with God read this book. As I read through the opening chapter I immediately felt the presence of God on every line. If you are going through a dark night of the soul right now, [In the Secret Place] will help you to reconnect and refocus on who you are in Christ and your purpose for being here. It is all about Him, knowing Him, loving Him, and being close to Him. I have read many books pertaining to this topic, but I love the way that Priscar has presented it at such a level that even the newest baby Christians can read it and immediately apply it to their personal walk and growth in relationship with God. So buy a copy for yourself and buy copies to give away to others to encourage them. Blessings to you, Priscar, for a wonderful book.

Pastor Rosalind Anglin
England

But thou, when thou
prayest , enter into thy
closet, and when thou hast
shut thy door, pray to thy
Father which is in secret;
and thy Father which seeth
in secret shall reward thee
openly

Matthew 6:6

Dedication

I dedicate this book to my nephew, Marvin Joshua, whose name means "Great Lord Jehovah is salvation." You are a great joy and love to all of us, your family. Time is going so fast. Soon you will be a grown man with a purpose. My prayer is that God will draw you unto Himself and grant you wisdom. I love you!

Synopsis

The purpose of *In the Secret Place: Conversations with God* is to help us revel in the presence of the Lord. This book is written to inspire us to set time aside to enter into the Secret Place of the Most High God. Only there will we find protection under His shadow from the troubles and persecutions in this present world. However tight our schedules may be, we can overcome the world's pressures by daily visiting the Secret Place. Ultimately, we will find ourselves yearning to go to there. I pray that this book inspires you and highlights the importance of waiting at the feet of Jesus.

Gratitude

I thank the Lord for making me worthy of this revelation. This book was birthed out of the prompting of the Holy Spirit. I did not expect to come up with this message. It is true that whomever God calls He equips. "He who does not love me will not obey my teaching. These words you hear are not my own; they belong to the Father who sent me. All this I have spoken while still with you. But the Counselor, the Holy Spirit, whom the Father will send in my name, will teach you all things and will remind you of everything I have said to you. Peace I leave with you; my peace I give you. I do not give to you as the world gives. Do not let your hearts be troubled and do not be afraid" (John 14:24–27 NIV).

Psalm 91

He that dwelleth in the secret place of the most High shall abide under the shadow of the Almighty. I will say of the LORD, He is my refuge and my fortress: my God; in him will I trust. Surely he shall deliver thee from the snare of the fowler, and from the noisome pestilence. He shall cover thee with his feathers, and under his wings shalt thou trust: his truth shall be thy shield and buckler. Thou shalt not be afraid for the terror by night; nor for the arrow that flieth by day; Nor for the pestilence that walketh in darkness; nor for the destruction that wasteth at noonday. A thousand shall fall at thy side, and ten thousand at thy right hand; but it shall not come nigh thee. Only with thine eyes shalt thou behold and see the reward of the wicked. Because thou hast made the LORD, which is my refuge, even the most High, thy habitation; there shall no evil befall thee, neither shall any plague come nigh thy dwelling. For he shall give his angels charge over thee, to keep thee in all thy ways. They shall bear thee up in their hands, lest thou dash thy foot against a stone. Thou shalt tread upon the lion and adder: the young lion and the dragon shalt thou trample under feet. Because he hath set his love upon me, therefore will I deliver him: I will set him on high, because he hath known my name. He shall call upon me, and I will answer him: I will be with him in trouble; I will deliver him, and honour him. With long life will I satisfy him, and shew him my salvation.

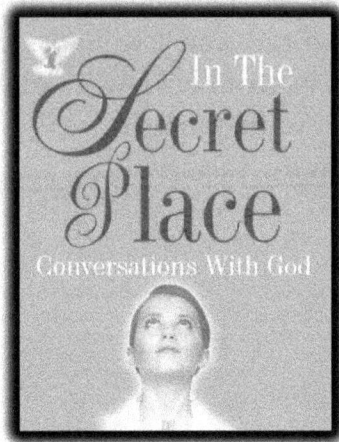

In The
Secret Place
Conversations With God

The atmosphere of worship enables us to express our devotion to God. While in it, the bruises we have incurred are being healed without even having to utter a word to our Heavenly Father.

Contents

Thou calledst in trouble, and I delivered thee; I answered thee in the secret place of thunder: I proved thee at the waters of Meribah. Selah. Hear, O my people, and I will testify unto thee: O Israel, if thou wilt hearken unto me; There shall no strange god be in thee; neither shalt thou worship any strange god. I am the LORD thy God, which brought thee out of the land of Egypt: open thy mouth wide, and I will fill it.

Psalm 81:7–10

Chapter One

Who to Trust?

A secret is something that is kept hidden from knowledge or view. It is information that is confidentially shared to the trusted few. It is often quite difficult to find someone who is completely trustworthy and reliable to keep a secret. Some things we share are to be kept confidential. Sometimes we share things that are mysteries to us, perhaps beyond ordinary understanding—for example, information that is precious to us. Others may want to share secrets with us. A secret is not shared with everyone. It can be a heartache, question, encouragement, instruction, enlightenment, or even a method or formula on which success is based.

In this day and age, it is hard for one to confide without being judged. Many people have tried to be transparent as they open their hearts to others but have been wounded and attacked. Thus they have rejected anything to do with fellowship. We need to be sensitive and careful how we relate to others. Our conversations should be focused on building and uplifting fellow brethren rather than downgrading them.

A fellow believer told me a mistake that another believer had committed several years ago. Although this other believer had probably changed and may have repented, he was still being condemned for past deeds. Sometimes the person we judge actually has a closer relationship with the Lord than we who consider ourselves to be righteous. It is written in the Scripture that we are to think of pure things that are praiseworthy. "Finally, brethren, whatsoever things are true, whatsoever things are honest, whatsoever things are just, whatsoever things are pure, whatsoever things are lovely, whatsoever things are of good report; if there be any virtue, and if there be any praise, think on these things" (Phil. 4:8).

Shooting our wounded contradicts the teachings of Christ. He said we must be our brother's keeper. It hurts when people leave a church or ministry because they have been humiliated by the ministry team. Some complain that their confidential information or matters have been made public without their consent. Imagine this all too familiar and shocking scenario: A church member goes to a pastor or elder for counseling and prayer, hoping to find help in resolving a problem, but instead they learn that the contents of their discussion have found its way into the pulpit in a sermon. Lack of confidentiality has contributed to many "falling short" or living in sin because they cannot open up to their shepherds and share the difficulties they face in their walk for fear of being humiliated in public.

Medical caregivers are sworn to patient confidentiality. A patient's information would never at any time be made public. If it becomes necessary that the patient's data be disclosed, the doctor must seek the patient's permission.

Our bodies are the temple of God. When we congregate together, we form a fellowship. A church is not a building but the gathering of the brethren to form a fellowship. In these fellowships are different types of people, some who have issues and believe that God, through His servant (pastors, teachers, elders), will help them overcome. The majority are a wounded people seeking help. Others are sick physically, emotionally, or spiritually. If we, the body of Christ, would apply this principle of keeping confidences and helping others overcome their difficulties, then many would not be hopping from one church or ministry to another. Though we live in a transient society, it would be constructive if church members would remain in a church at least three to five years before moving to another church or ministry.

For all who are either wounded or find it difficult to trust anyone, it is advisable to rediscover their first love with the Lord. The need to reconnect or reaffirm their commitment to the Lord is imperative. Where a human touch cannot reach, the Lord's hand is never too short. We can do this by finding a particular place where we can be at peace and speak words of reflection to the Lord God. This place can be either a dedicated place, a room in your house, or even in a peaceful garden or park. This place is where we can be alone for a while. We should meditate upon the paths of life experienced to this point, and note the Lord's footprints carrying us throughout. We need to realize again that had it not been for the Lord who was on our side, the Enemy would have swallowed us alive. "The

LORD redeemeth the soul of his servants: and none of them that trust in him shall be desolate" (Ps. 34:22).

Every Christian needs to make time to visit what I refer to as the Secret Place. This is where we find solace from disappointment and heartache. In the Secret Place we create an atmosphere that makes room for the presence of God to emerge. Only in the presence of God can we find comfort and peace.

The Secret Place is dedicated for time alone with God. It is where we can be utterly truthful with the Lord. We open our hearts' desires and trust the Lord for direction. Here we are free from the fear of being judged. In this place we understand that God knows everything before we even speak to Him. Nevertheless, God loves to hear us talking to Him. This is a place of acceptance and contentment. For those who know this place, they long for it whenever they are away from it. It is a precious, holy place of quietness and peace.

It is a sorely needed place of fellowship where we let God be our Abba: Father. We let Him hold us in His presence and wipe away our tears. When he does, pain fades and disappears. As they say regarding the reality TV shows: This isn't just reality, it is actuality. There is no holding back! Emotional wounds are healed. Restoration is here. Rejection is gone. We are accepted for who we are and not for what people want us to be for their selfish motives. Trust and acknowledgment is in this place. Close your eyes and receive the peace of the Lord that is descending upon you now as we pray.

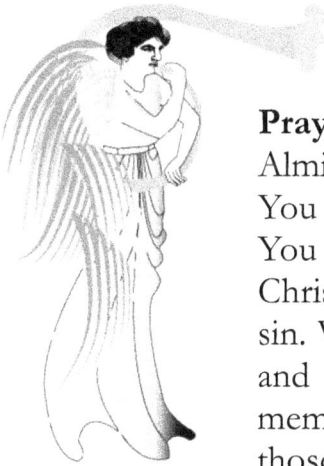

Prayer
Almighty God, our Father, You loved us so much that You sent Your Son, Jesus Christ, to redeem us from sin. When we feel betrayed and wounded by family members or friends or by those who have been placed in authority over us in school, at work, or in places of worship, may You heal our wounded emotions.

continued . . .

For some of us, it is difficult to even talk about certain matters because no one will believe us. Threats have been made, vindictive words have been spoken, yet, Lord God, we know and believe that You are above them all. You taught us to respect authority and obey our parents; but some of us feel let down. Father God, may You wipe away the pain and the tears of the person who is reading this book right now in the name of Jesus Christ, Your dear Son. Amen.

Chapter Two

The Blood of Jesus

As I write this, memories flood my mind of how many wonderful things God has done for me. Indeed, sometimes I am convinced that I am the most loved person by God. You, too, may feel especially blessed by God. Since I received the call from God to serve Him, I have experienced tragedies that could have taken my life, but somehow I still exist. This process has been a time of purification and a period of training. Just like soldiers go through basic training so that they can be of service to their nations, Christians, too, pass through spiritual training that helps us exercise the power in the name of Jesus Christ.

This, in the end, brings full understanding to us that there is nothing on this earth as powerful as the blood of Jesus and His name. I can't help but marvel regarding the places and the people I have encountered in my life. Some were sent by God as angels who strengthened me either through provision of some sort or by their intercession. When Elijah escaped from Jezebel, God sent His angel to him. Jezebel was angry with Elijah because he believed in the only true and living God, and he had gotten rid of Baal's prophets. Jezebel was indeed a messenger from hell whose mission was to cause destruction. However, Elijah was not alone as he mistakenly imagined. He had an angel assigned to him (not to mention the remnant of 7,000 in Israel who had not bowed to Baal; see I Kings 19:18).

Though we may feel that God is not concerned with us, the Bible states that He will not allow the sun to smite us by day nor the moon by night. God will always reveal to us what the Enemy is planning against us.

One day I was facing difficult emotional battles. I wondered whether God was truly aware. In my spirit I heard two Scriptures: "I will never leave you nor forsake you." I then heard again, "And lo, I am with you always." If we are honest and reflect on every hard time we have experienced, I believe we can actually be grateful for those moments, for they help shape our destinies.

What we thought was important then

become less significant, and the things we want are no longer desire. In fact, we may now be thankful that God did not allow certain things to happen. Such occasions have motivated us to spend extra time with God and to be even more focused in prayer. We have learned the Word of God intensively during this period by surfing from one page of the Bible to the next, searching for Scriptures that relate to or highlight our current predicament. We know what Scripture to quote and have come to know that the Bible is the true Word of God because we have put it to the test.

One day my neighbor in London claimed that he had out-of-body experiences. He was describing them to me as if they were something of which to be proud. I felt the conversation to be weird; I did not want to listen any further, so I cut him short by telling him that I am a Christian and our faith does not permit humans to do what is contrary to the Word of God. Believe me, that was a revelatory moment in which God enabled me to see clearly who was living next to me. It was the grace of God that preserved me. It took a couple of years for me to realize that obstacles were in every project I initiated. Nothing was working out they way I had planned.

The anointing from God is like a hidden treasure. Only those who continue to persistently search will receive it. Your perseverance and quest for God's plan in your life will lead you to the purpose God has for you. Each of us has something special for which we were imparted at birth. We can all come to full realization of whatever that is if we spend time in the Secret Place.

Here we learn and receive instruction concerning the next move toward which God is ushering us. It is also where we receive instruction regarding whom to connect with or disconnect from. It is a place where selfish desires and ungodly ambitions are pruned from our lives. It is at this place that every other false voice is silenced. With full understanding, we overcome the Enemy by the blood of the Lamb and the word of our testimony. Knowing fully, as is written in the Bible, that only the counsel of the Lord God shall stand.

> Remember the former things of old: for I am God, and there is none else; I am God, and there is none like me, Declaring the end from the beginning, and from ancient times the things that are not yet done, saying, My counsel shall stand, and I will do all my pleasure: Calling a ravenous bird from the

> east, the man that executeth my counsel
> from a far country: yea, I have spoken it, I
> will also bring it to pass; I have purposed it,
> I will also do it. Hearken unto me, ye
> stouthearted, that are far from righ-
> teousness: I bring near my righteousness; it
> shall not be far off, and my salvation shall
> not tarry: and I will place salvation in Zion
> for Israel, my glory." (Isaiah 46:9–13)

Much spiritual warfare was battling around me. The same neighbor was often inquisitive about my affairs and my plans for the day. He was insistent to know my business. One day it occurred to me that this person never revealed much about himself but managed to pry a good deal of information from me. This was possible because, for a while, I felt a bit indebted to him. When I was ill, neighbors and friends took care of me, and he was there occasionally with kind words. As a result I came to think of him as a good person. I appreciated the help. What I didn't realize was that Satan's forces can deceive us under the guise of kindness. He was there to test my strength and faith in God. It was time to find out whether I could pass the test. While I was going through this, the words of a woman of God stated years before kept recurring in my mind: "If you pass the test, you will receive the crown. Whenever I go through tough times and feel like giving up, I hear that voice challenging me to continue on. This message helps to keep me grounded and focused. This clearly shows how much God loves us and is willing to speak to us if we would but listen and obey.

We come to understand that only the blood of Jesus Christ can make us clean. While others are trusting in other sources for protection, we Christians depend on the name of Jesus Christ, knowing His blood is more powerful than a million forces that might come against us. For this reason we very much need to carve out time from our busy schedules to be in the Secret Place so that we can be renewed. We need strength that is the joy of the Lord, and this is experienced through fellowship with Him. We then gain full knowledge that it is not by might, nor by power, but by the Spirit of the Lord (Zech 4:6). When we receive bad news, we still have confidence that God will make a way for us, for the Word of God is true, and all things work together for good to them that love God and are called according to His purpose in Christ Jesus (Rom. 8:28).

God instructed Moses to tell the

Israelites to apply blood to their doorposts so that when the angel of death passed by, they would not be affected, and so God was true to His Word. "For the LORD will pass through to smite the Egyptians; and when he seeth the blood upon the lintel, and on the two side posts, the LORD will pass over the door, and will not suffer the destroyer to come in unto your houses to smite you" (Ex. 12:23). Yet the Lord's blood accomplishes much more. "For this is my blood of the new testament, which is shed for many for the remission of sins" (Matt. 26:28). It becomes clear that our righteousness through Christ Jesus has brought us closer to God. We are able to approach God because our sins are hidden under the blood of Jesus. "But now in Christ Jesus ye who sometimes were far off are made nigh by the blood of Christ" (Eph. 2:13).

Let us plead the blood of Jesus against every plan of the Enemy that is contrary to the will of God for us, with full knowledge that we are more than conquerors through Christ Jesus who strengthens us (Rom. 8:37).

Prayer

God Jehovah Nissi, our Father, we come to You in the name of Jesus Christ. Many are still struggling to understand the power in the blood of Jesus Christ. Some had knowledge, but this has been stolen from them by the Enemy through false doctrine.

continued . . .

Due to this, these people lack confidence and they feel as if their lives are shattered. Their minds have been ruined because the Enemy is using them for his gain.

They have been made to put their trust in man-made objects, which they are given in every service for protection. They have been made to forget the power in the name of Jesus Christ. Indeed, the apostle Paul confronted this problem and was not afraid to deal with it. "O foolish Galatians, who hath bewitched you, that ye should not obey the truth, before whose eyes Jesus Christ hath been evidently set forth, crucified among you?" (Gal. 3:1). We pray, Father God, in the name of Jesus Christ, Your dear Son, set the minds of these people free from everything that is contrary to your Word.

continued . . .

We plead the blood of Jesus over our minds, on our loved ones, and upon our dwellings. We renounce every false initiation that has taken place, which has been caused either by lack of understanding or with half understanding. You said in Your Word that whoever is joined with Christ is one spirit with Him (1 Cor. 6:17).

You also said, "There is therefore now no condemnation to them which are in Christ Jesus, who walk not after the flesh, but after the Spirit" (Rom. 8:1). May Your light penetrate our minds as we cover ourselves in the blood of Jesus Christ. May our footsteps be ordered by You. We pray this in the name that is above every other name: the name of Jesus Christ. Amen.

Chapter Three

The Presence of God

Nothing is more important or valuable than being in God's presence. In the Secret Place we find protection and we are shielded from the devourer, who is roaming to and fro seeking whom to destroy (1 Peter 5:8). Satan is not bothered by empty vessels, because they are of no trouble to him. Lucifer is bothered by intercessors and worshippers: people who perceive the future and call it into existence as revealed to them by God while in the Secret Place. I am excited because I know God is able and never leaves unfinished business.

Intercessors who are also worshippers are not moved by hearsay—only by the presence of God. They have a direct connection with heaven. When they hear something, they don't wander, seeking clarification from flesh and blood. Whether bad or good news, they take it as their responsibility to intercede for God's will to be done. They understand that they have been given power to root out that which has not been orchestrated by God, to destroy it, and to plant and build God's kingdom here on earth. Jeremiah 1:10 states: "See, I have this day set thee over the nations and over the kingdoms, to root out, and to pull down, and to destroy, and to throw down, to build, and to plant." These are people who have been groomed by God while spending time in His presence at the Secret Place; they know the voice of God. They can distinguish between what is false and what is true. They know that many claim to have heard from God, but whether God really spoke to them is another matter altogether.

These individuals are wise because they spend no time in argument or debate. They clearly understand that all the answers can be found in the Secret Place. They have full knowledge that truth as revealed by God is our shield. They have been given power by God and they know how to exercise it according to the Word of God. They are not biased or partial. Their thinking is not based on some tribe or nation of origin. They are kingdom thinkers with understanding that eventually all nations, all tribes, and all people shall come together as one to worship the Almighty God.

This kind of understanding can be achieved only while nestled in the Secret Place.

> He that dwelleth in the secret place of the most High shall abide under the shadow of the Almighty. I will say of the LORD, He is my refuge and my fortress: my God; in him will I trust. Surely he shall deliver thee from the snare of the fowler, and from the noisome pestilence. He shall cover thee with his feathers, and under his wings shalt thou trust: his truth shall be thy shield and buckler. (Psalm 91:1–4)

As I mentioned earlier, the conversation that my neighbor had with me became very useful later on as I gained wisdom. It is true that we serve an amazing God! He made sure that some knowledge of what was happening around me was not fully revealed until the appointed time. God can disclose to us only as much as we're able to handle at any given time or in any circumstance. He takes us through different stages while simultaneously preparing us.

When we pass each level of testing, we graduate to a higher level of maturity. As a result of what happened a year or so after that conversation, I was grateful that God did not allow me to have full knowledge or understanding of what the man was saying at the time. Had this been the case, I would have been terrified because I was not fully prepared.

With lack of knowledge we often tremble when dark thunderheads hover over our lives. The purpose of the Word of God is to equip us, to make the giant in us rise and take its full place in our homes and surroundings. Only when we are consistently waiting on God and studying His Word in the Secret Place will we comprehend the power that has been given to us as it is written in Luke 10:18–21:

> And he said unto them, I beheld Satan as lightning fall from heaven. Behold, I give unto you power to tread on serpents and scorpions, and over all the power of the enemy: and nothing shall by any means hurt you. Notwithstanding in this rejoice not, that the spirits are subject unto you; but rather rejoice, because your names are written in heaven. In that hour Jesus rejoiced in spirit, and said, I thank thee, O Father, Lord of heaven and earth, that thou hast hid these things from the wise and prudent, and hast revealed them unto babes: even so, Father; for so it seemed good in thy sight.

However, as the whole picture gradually revealed itself later, I was grateful to God. It was clear that He had protected me so that He could practically prepare me while in His Secret Place. He enabled me to realize that we are protected and are more powerful than the forces of darkness if we are in Christ. I felt more powerful when I came to realize that though I was surrounded by forces that were messengers of darkness, they could not touch me. These forces were international and of different backgrounds. They were angry with me for being a Christian. They were much troubled by my faith. Sometimes they would ask me why I was a Christian. And when we prayed in tongues, they grew very upset! It was a spiritual battle—a good ground on which to exercise the power that is inherent in the name and the blood of Jesus Christ.

Nevertheless, I told them I was a Christian and nobody can do about it. It is final. I was alone and a woman against seven or eight men. One day when I was praying, I heard that the neighbor who once spoke to me about the out-of-body experiences had become very agitated and fled his place. He never came back till the following day to collect his belongings. Within a week, he had completely moved out. A few months later, the remaining two moved out in the same manner. Throughout this period, I never did anything wrong to any of them. They left purely for the reason that I am a Christian. We have heard of persecution against Christians in different countries, but sometimes it happens right under our noses. I wondered how I managed to live in the same place for more than three years with such people. I survived because Christ in me is the hope of glory (Col. 1:27). I have fought many battles that I could not have won without Him.

The Enemy can try but he cannot harm us if we are in the Secret Place. One time I seemed to see two gigantic angels chasing something out of my place, though I had no idea what it was. This incident enlightened me that angels are assigned to protect me. My sharing this is to help you understand that no battle is too big for God. For example, a person contemplating suicide to escape overwhelming problems must know that ending his or her life will not bring resolution. Rather, it would only keep him or her far from the presence of God.

The fortunate ones, those leading a righteous life in Christ Jesus, are destined for heaven, where the throne of God is, in His presence. The person without Christ who commits suicide is destined to go to hell, which is for eternity. Right this moment the Lord is calling you; He is stretching out His hand to you. The Lord feels your pain, and Christ wants you to take hold of His hand so that He can lead you to the Secret Place of the Most High God. In that place you will be protected.

Always remember that fear of the unknown is not the portion of believers. We have a sound mind of power and of love. We do not worry about tomorrow, for it will take care of itself. We must consecrate ourselves because sin cuts us off from the presence of God. Adam and Eve hid from God when they heard Him walking in the garden. "And they heard the voice of the LORD God walking in the garden in the cool of the day: and Adam and his wife hid themselves from the presence of the LORD God amongst the trees of the garden" (Gen. 3:8).

We, too, need to understand that sin causes us to run away from God. As we continue in sin, the distance keeps widening.

Eventually, we may end up in major trouble.

Moses understood how important it was to involve God in every decision we make in life. He dealt with God regarding day-to-day activities that concerned the Israelites. When the Hebrews complained about food, Moses took the matter to God. It is impossible to converse with God unless one is allowed access into His presence. Moses' daily life was dependent upon consultation with God. Undoubtedly, Moses serves as an excellent example of how much God is concerned about the very details of our lives.

> And Moses said unto the LORD, See, thou sayest unto me, Bring up this people: and thou hast not let me know whom thou wilt send with me. Yet thou hast said, I know thee by name, and thou hast also found grace in my sight. Now therefore, I pray thee, if I have found grace in thy sight, shew me now thy way, that I may know thee, that I may find grace in thy sight: and consider that this nation is thy people. And he said, My presence shall go with thee, and I will give thee rest. And he said unto him, If thy presence go not with me, carry us not up hence. (Exodus 33:12–15)

Yes, fullness of joy and pleasure is found

in the presence of God. Psalm 16:11 reads: "Thou wilt shew me the path of life: in thy presence is fullness of joy; at thy right hand there are pleasures forevermore." Singing, dancing, and praising occurs in His presence. No flesh shall ever glory in themselves in His presence.

> For ye see your calling, brethren, how that not many wise men after the flesh, not many mighty, not many noble, are called: But God hath chosen the foolish things of the world to confound the wise; and God hath chosen the weak things of the world to confound the things which are mighty; And base things of the world, and things which are despised, hath God chosen, yea, and things which are not, to bring to nought things that are. That no flesh should glory in his presence. But of him are ye in Christ Jesus, who of God is made unto us wisdom, and righteousness, and sanctification, and redemption: That, according as it is written, He that glorieth, let him glory in the Lord. (1 Corinthians 1:26–31)

May knowledge and revelation be imparted to us.

Prayer

Lord God, Creator of the universe, You spoke to Abraham and Moses as Your friends. These two men were able to intercede for their nation because they had access to Your presence. You spoke with them and led them through their journey to the Promised Land. They never doubted Your Word at any given time. They are an example to us. Many of us have hopes, dreams, and promises that we believe You spoke to us. Yet we are stuck and doubts fill our minds. May You help us to walk by faith as these two great servants and the other men and women of faith did as recorded in Hebrew 11:3–13. May we experience Your presence as we seek Your face. We pray this in the name of Jesus Christ. Amen.

Chapter Four

More Time Is Needed

We could be successful in every aspect of life if we spend more time in the Secret Place, where secrets are revealed and where knowledge is imparted. Doubts and fear are wiped out of our minds. It is a place of possibilities, of transaction and fellowship. This is where we become intimate with God. All the masks come off. In this place we receive architectural plans from the realm of the spirit on forthcoming businesses and God's desire for us of which few have captured. It is a place of revelation. While here, we can express ourselves without fear of being judged. It is a precious place; I long for it.

We read from the Scripture that those who fear God are trusted with His secrets.

> The secret of the LORD is with them that fear him; and he will shew them his covenant. Mine eyes are ever toward the LORD; for he shall pluck my feet out of the net. Turn thee unto me, and have mercy upon me; for I am desolate and afflicted.

43

> The troubles of my heart are enlarged: O bring thou me out of my distresses. Look upon mine affliction and my pain; and forgive all my sins. Consider mine enemies; for they are many; and they hate me with cruel hatred. O keep my soul, and deliver me: let me not be ashamed; for I put my trust in thee. (Psalm 25:14–20)

Remaining in the Secret Place can appear lonely and isolated to some who lack understanding. On the contrary, you will have a good time in the presence of the Most High God. While here, you can converse audibly with God and understand why David danced till his clothes dropped! His wife, Michal, thought he was a mental case, but he was only worshipping transparently God, whom he adored.

> And as the ark of the LORD came into the city of David, Michal Saul's daughter looked through a window, and saw king David leaping and dancing before the LORD; and she despised him in her heart.
>
> And they brought in the ark of the LORD, and set it in his place, in the midst of the tabernacle that David had pitched for it: and David offered burnt offerings and peace offerings before the LORD. And as soon as David had made an end of offering burnt offerings and peace

offerings, he blessed the people in the name of the LORD of hosts. And he dealt among all the people, even among the whole multitude of Israel, as well to the women as men, to every one a cake of bread, and a good piece of flesh, and a flagon of wine. So all the people departed every one to his house. Then David returned to bless his household. And Michal the daughter of Saul came out to meet David, and said, How glorious was the king of Israel today, who uncovered himself today in the eyes of the handmaids of his servants, as one of the vain fellows shamelessly uncovereth himself! And David said unto Michal, It was before the LORD, which chose me before thy father, and before all his house, to appoint me ruler over the people of the LORD, over Israel: therefore will I play before the LORD. And I will yet be more vile than thus, and will be base in mine own sight: and of the maidservants which thou hast spoken of, of them shall I be had in honour. Therefore Michal the daughter of Saul had no child unto the day of her death. (2 Samuel 6 16–23)

Michal was concerned about her husband's public image. As a royal princess, perhaps she was convinced that royalty is required to have a dignified image. She could not understand why David and the people were so happy and danced as they did. Possibly, some of us can understand or relate to David in this circumstance. While dancing, he was probably recalling every good thing that God had done for him. He was passionately grateful to God, who had taken a shepherd boy that even his own family despised and had honored him beyond belief. Or maybe he was praising a God whose everlastingly kind and holy character he had come to love.

We need always to reflect on and show our gratitude to God even for allowing these old bodies to crawl out of bed each morning. When I was ill, I lay on the hospital bed for over a month. I could not stand on my own, let alone walk. I had to be supported. I was not sure whether I would ever be able to walk again. While lying there, I would look at the people passing outside my door and ask myself whether they knew how blessed they were just to be able to walk.

We sometimes mourn over every little thing that doesn't go like we want, and we crave so heartily, yet we forget that just to be able to walk is a miracle. We should not take good health for granted. Whatever high positions we may hold in society, let's not allow such to obstruct us in worshipping our Maker. David was king of Israel! Yet he danced for the Lord till some of his clothing fell off. If we would train ourselves to be humble before the Lord no matter what life throws at us, there is nothing that God will not bless us with or see us through. As we learn how to appreciate God in every 'little' thing He does for us, He will bless us even more. This is possible if we don't allow people or possessions to become idols in our lives.

"The secret things belong unto the LORD our God: but those things which are revealed belong unto us and to our children forever, that we may do all the words of this law" (Deut. 29:29). While in this place, we also come to realize that however much is revealed to us by God not every bit of information is to be shared publicly. "Happy is the man that findeth wisdom, and the man that getteth understanding" (Prov. 3:13). While Christ was with the disciples, Moses and Elijah appeared during the transfiguration, and Jesus charged them, saying, "Tell the vision to no man" (Matt. 17:9). According to the Scripture, the Lord mentioned this to them as they were coming down the mountain. This signifies they were coming from the presence of God. It was a Secret Place! Therefore, it could imply that whatever is revealed to us in the Secret Place we need to weigh with the help of the Holy Spirit and decide how much is to be disclosed.

> And after six days Jesus taketh Peter, James, and John his brother, and bringeth them up into an high mountain apart, And was transfigured before them: and his face did shine as the sun, and his raiment was white as the light. And, behold, there appeared unto them Moses and Elias talking with him. Then answered Peter, and said unto Jesus, Lord, it is good for us to be here: if thou wilt, let us make here three tabernacles; one for thee, and one for Moses, and one for Elias. While he yet spake, behold, a bright cloud overshadowed them: and behold a voice out of the cloud, which said, This is my beloved Son, in whom I am well pleased; hear ye him.
>
> And when the disciples heard it, they fell on their face, and were sore afraid. And Jesus came and touched them, and said, Arise, and be not afraid. And when they had lifted up their eyes, they saw no man, save Jesus only. And as they came down from the mountain, Jesus charged them, saying, Tell the vision to no man, until the Son of man be risen again from the dead. (Matthew 17:1–9)

As we spend more time in the Secret

Place, we become familiar with His voice. Intimacy with the Lord grows deeper as more time is dedicated to it. We learn in the Scripture that when Samuel was a young boy he heard a voice calling his name three times, which he thought to have been Eli's. However, as Samuel matured under the training of Eli, the high priest, he came to well recognize God's voice. "And he ran unto Eli, and said, Here am I; for thou calledst me. And he said, I called not; lie down again. And he went and lay down" (1 Sam. 3:5). Samuel grew into a respected prophet. "And Samuel grew, and the LORD was with him, and did let none of his words fall to the ground" (1 Sam. 3:19).

The mightier works achieved by the apostles were due to the time spent with the Lord. From the moment Peter and his brother heard Christ's call, they stayed with Him till His death and resurrection. As a result, their ministries had great impact—one that affected the entire planet. The Lord said to His disciples, "Greater works shall ye do" (John 14:12). While in the presence of the Lord, we need to understand that we are to worship Him. When the Lord visited Mary and Martha, Martha was busy with necessary labours. But she failed to understand that waiting and learning at the feet of Jesus Christ was more crucial. Her sister, Mary, left every other important matter to make herself available to sit at the feet of Jesus, the Messiah.

None of the walks and works we do for ministry or the church will be successful or have any impact if we fail to understand the importance of waiting on the Lord. Whether a minister or an ordinary Christian, we should all set aside time to be in the Secret Place.

Our businesses, ministries, or families rely on us as a voice of wisdom for direction. We can give only what we possess. The disciples said to the man at the gate that though they had no silver and gold, they could offer him the power to walk in the name of Jesus Christ. We also can determine how successful we are by the spiritual impact we have through the power of Christ. Only then will the world know that we are called from darkness into the marvellous light to spend time with the Lord in His presence. You can be light and salt to the hurting world. Will you?

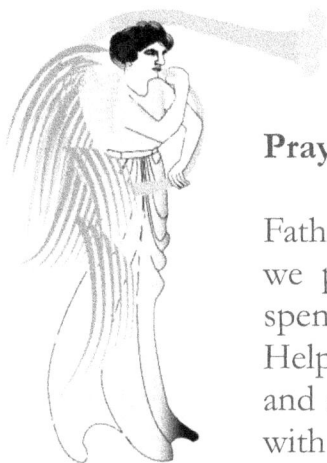

Prayer

Father, in Christ's mighty Name we pray that You enable us to spend more time with You. Help us to prioritize our time and seek more of You. We plead with You to remove those things that we think are more important than You. Help us to see clearly that in You we find the answers we have been searching for in all the wrong places. Your Word reads: "Blessed are they which do hunger and thirst after righteousness: for they shall be filled" (Matt. 5:6). In Jesus' powerful Name we pray. Amen.

Chapter Five

The Voice of God

In the Secret Place we learn how to hear the voice of God in a different dimension. When Elijah was instructed to climb atop the mountain so that God could visit him, he did not know in what form God would appear. He had to pay attention so that he could clearly distinguish between a strong wind, an earthquake, a fire, and eventually a still, small voice. Perhaps he was surprised to find God speaking in such a gentle, soft voice.

> And he said, Go forth, and stand upon the mount before the LORD. And, behold, the LORD passed by, and a great and *strong wind* rent the mountains, and brake in pieces the rocks before the LORD; but the LORD was not in the wind: and after the wind an *earthquake*; but the LORD was not in the earthquake: And after the earthquake a *fire*; but the LORD was not in the fire: and after the fire a *still small voice*. And it was so, when Elijah heard it that he wrapped his face in his mantle, and went out, and stood in the

> entering in of the cave. And, behold, there came a voice unto him, and said, What doest thou here, Elijah? (1 Kings 19:11–13)

The prophet took responsibility to identify through which of the many voices God was speaking. When people try to persuade you to do things that you are not convicted to do, you must find confirmation in the Secret Place. Withdraw from the crowd and make your way to the Secret Place, where answers and clarity resides. Anyone can hear from God if he or she is willing to do what it takes to activate an open dialogue with heaven.

Staying focused on godliness is an attribute that contributes to heavenly access. It is written that, without holiness, no one can see God. "Follow peace with all men, and holiness, without which no man shall see the Lord" (Heb. 12:14). God listens to every one of us if we walk uprightly and make time to converse with Him. The Secret Place is where you worship God with songs of praise, Bible study, or simply sitting still. Sometimes we go there just to laugh with God and have fellowship. It is an amazing place! We have already learned that God instructed Elijah to go to the top of a mountain so He could speak to him. This same

God has feelings just like we do. He feels our joy and our sorrow as well. When we reject Him, He withdraws. God does not force Himself on us. He would rather we approach Him willingly.

Because of divine intervention while Moses lived in the desert, He became the leader of the Hebrew nation. He was a blessed man who spent most of his time in the presence of God. "And Moses said, I will now turn aside, and see this great sight, why the bush is not burnt" (Ex. 3:3). In that state, he was able to receive instructions and strategies that helped him deliver the Israelites from Egypt. Most of us know that his task was challenging, and God almost aborted His plan in the wilderness when the Hebrews rebelled against God. It came to a point where God was fed up and wanted to finish the Israelites in the wilderness. Simultaneously, God promised to start a new nation through Moses!

It becomes obvious here what an unselfish man of God Moses was. If he were selfish and self-righteous, he might have encouraged God to destroy His rebellious people and start a new nation through him. But he refused to think about any ambitions he might have had and pleaded with God to spare the Israelites. It is important that we see how useful it is for each of us to be knowledgeable in the Word of God. Moses reminded God of His own words when He made a promise to the Israelites. Moses' mind was on what would happen to the 'reputation' of God among the Egyptians if He destroyed the Israelites in the wilderness.

> And the LORD said unto Moses, How long will this people provoke me? and how long will it be ere they believe me, for all the signs which I have shewed among them? I will smite them with the pestilence, and disinherit them, and will make of thee a greater nation and mightier than they. And Moses said unto the LORD, Then the Egyptians shall hear it, (for thou broughtest up this people in thy might from among them;) And they will tell it to the inhabitants of this land: for they have heard that thou LORD art among this people, that thou LORD art seen face to face, and that thy cloud standeth over them, and that thou goest before them, by day time in a pillar of a cloud, and in a pillar of fire by night. Now if thou shalt kill all this people as one man, then the nations which have heard the fame of thee will speak, saying, Because the LORD was not able to bring this people into the land which he sware unto them, therefore

> he hath slain them in the wilderness.
> (Numbers 14 :11–16)

While in the Secret Place, we should also intercede on behalf of those who are in need, for men and women of God, for every man, woman, and child who needs God's intervention, just as Moses did while in the presence of God.

> And now, I beseech thee, let the power of my LORD be great, according as thou hast spoken, saying, The LORD is longsuffering, and of great mercy, forgiving iniquity and transgression, and by no means clearing the guilty, visiting the iniquity of the fathers upon the children unto the third and fourth generation. Pardon, I beseech thee, the iniquity of this people according unto the greatness of thy mercy, and as thou hast forgiven this people, from Egypt even until now. And the LORD said, I have pardoned according to thy word: But as truly as I live, all the earth shall be filled with the glory of the LORD. (Numbers 14:17–21)

The Holy Spirit is a great revealer and an unfailing messenger. If we cooperate with Him, He will tell us who needs help and where to find that person. Moses referred God to His own Word: 'according as thou hast spoken'.

Moses was depicted later by Christ as one who emphasized the importance of applying the Word of God in difficult situations.

> And [Satan] saith unto him, If thou be the Son of God, cast thyself down: for it is written, He shall give his angels charge concerning thee: and in their hands they shall bear thee up, lest at any time thou dash thy foot against a stone. Jesus said unto him, It is written again, Thou shalt not tempt the Lord thy God. Again, the devil taketh him up into an exceeding high mountain, and sheweth him all the kingdoms of the world, and the glory of them; And saith unto him, All these things will I give thee, if thou wilt fall down and worship me. Then saith Jesus unto him, Get thee hence, Satan: for it is written, Thou shalt worship the Lord thy God, and him only shalt thou serve. (Matthew 4:6–10)

A man once told me that he had been called at an early age to ministry. According to him, all was well in the beginning. Unfortunately, things turned different in the later years. He said he was so much on fire for God that he neglected himself and his own family. As a young husband, he did not achieve a wise balance between ministry and family life. This, according to him, led to a divorce after almost two decades of marriage. Apart from attending church occasionally and assisting with light duties, he is no longer in ministry. His flame of zeal burned out. He told me that now when he sees young people on fire for God, he tells them to slow down so they can enjoy their lives first. He advises them that all will be there waiting for them in the future.

We would likely agree that this man appears to have thrown the baby out with the bathwater. Just because his spiritual enthusiasm led to an imbalanced life does not mean others should completely quench the flame. This is where it is important that we understand the voice and the Word of God. The Word helps us weigh the voices speaking to us in order to know which one is of God.

As written in the Bible: "For the word of God is quick, and powerful, and sharper than any two-edged sword, piercing even to the dividing asunder of soul and spirit, and of the joints and marrow, and is a discerner of the thoughts and intents of the heart" (Heb. 4:12). All this can be achieved if we enter into the Secret Place regularly as did Moses and Christ.

Prayer

Father, we beseech Your help so that we would be able to recognize Your voice better. Help us shut down every other channel that is not flowing from You. When people come to us claiming that You have sent them, help us to discern and drink only from the pure fountain.

continued . .

Christ said: "My sheep hear my voice, and I know them, and they follow me: And I give unto them eternal life; and they shall never perish, neither shall any man pluck them out of my hand" (John 10:27–28). May You 'circumcise' our ears to hear only the voice of the Lord. Amen.

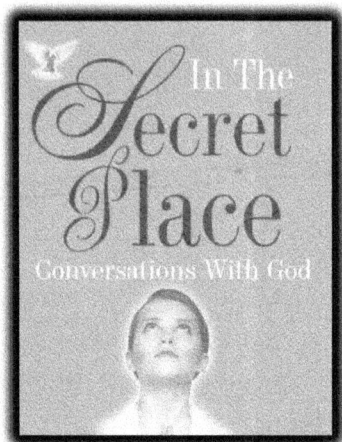

Thou shalt hide them in the secret
of thy presence from the pride of man:
thou shalt keep them secretly
in a pavilion from the strife of tongues.
Psalm 31:20

Chapter Six

Love

In the Secret Place we experience a fulfilling fellowship with our Maker. When this fellowship has grown deep, it will be noticeable. Our relationship with fellow brethren will begin to be more fulfilling and edifying. "If a man say, I love God, and hateth his brother, he is a liar: for he that loveth not his brother whom he hath seen, how can he love God whom he hath not seen?" (1 John 4:20).

Sadly, some believers claim to be filled with the Holy Spirit yet fail to extend even a warm welcome to others. I was in a meeting that some might refer to as a 'heavenly visitation' meeting. People were supposedly being filled with fire; I witnessed others jumping into the air and giving the impression of being totally filled with the Spirit. One would think that if the Lord were to show up in that moment, these people would be the first to be raptured!

When the meeting came to an end, many of these individuals crossed the room to their 'own kind,' refusing to interact with others. They segregated themselves into haughty groups. Apparently, some thought that they were more anointed or filled with the Holy Spirit than others. If a fellow believer cannot love brothers or sisters with *agape* love, how can such a person love God, whom they have not seen? Not only do ordinary Christians behave in this cold and unloving manner, ministers do as well. It grieves the Holy Spirit when one preaches a good message, just to ruin it with a negative word or attitude about another's ministry.

To experience the full manifestation of the presence of God in the Secret Place, we must make sure that our own houses are in order. To reach this level, we must have an understanding that our bodies are the temple of the Holy Spirit. There is a great need to be at peace with everyone as much as possible. Having done that allows us to have a direct channel of communication with God when we enter into the Secret Place. Love conquers a multitude of sins; this understanding helps us realize the need to forgive others and ourselves too. In the Scriptures, the Lord stated that if we approach the altar and remember that our brother has something against us, we need to go back to clear up the misunderstanding before we can proceed. (See Matthew 5:23–24.)

If this offer is rejected by that person, at least we have done our part. If we claim to be of God or to have known Him, then His attributes should begin to manifest through us. God is LOVE. "Beloved, let us love one another: for love is of God; and every one that loveth is born of God, and knoweth God" (1 John 4:7). Certainly we all need to understand this is not a one-time work of grace within us; rather, it is progressive. It is important for us to allow the Holy Spirit to modify us to reflect the image of God. If we stop resisting the Holy Spirit, He will begin His work in us. In other cases, we also need to stop hiding in the grace. We sometimes offend others or God intentionally and, in doing so, abuse the 'grace factor'. Truly, this walk of salvation that takes us to the Secret Place is by grace. We are saved by grace and we live each day by grace.

"For by grace you have been saved through faith, and that not of yourselves; it is the gift of God" (Eph. 2:8). In addition, Proverbs 9:10 states, "The fear of the LORD is the beginning of wisdom, And the knowledge of the Holy One is understanding." If we love and respect God, we will be careful of recurring offences that we thoughtlessly do toward others.

Wavering emotions and insecurity can be stabilized as we please God by fellowshipping with Him. Making a habit to be in the Secret Place will result in healing for our minds, bodies, and souls. When our emotions are imbalanced, we tend to allow them to rule us when making decisions. On the other hand, being insecure can stop one's progression either on a personal level, or in a career or ministry. When God fills us completely with the fruit of His Holy Spirit, such issues are dealt with starting from that point. The peace of God as promised by Christ takes over. The world becomes a 'new place'. Insecurity can contribute to one's holding grudges against others. When this happens, it is impossible for us to have a direct channel of communication with heaven. The Lord's Prayer becomes our highlight:

> After this manner therefore pray ye: Our Father which art in heaven, Hallowed be thy

name. Thy kingdom come. Thy will be done in earth, as it is in heaven. Give us this day our daily bread. And forgive us our debts, as we forgive our debtors. And lead us not into temptation, but deliver us from evil: For thine is the kingdom, and the power, and the glory, forever. Amen. For if ye forgive men their trespasses, your heavenly Father will also forgive you. (Matthew 6:9–14)

If we are honest, unforgiveness hinders breakthroughs for most of us. It is crystal clear that when we pray, we must make sure that we've forgiven those who have wronged us in order for us to also be forgiven; therefore, no amount of fasting, prayer, or good deeds can alter the Word of God as stated in the Lord's Prayer. This could be a contributing factor to some of the hindrances we experience. When misunderstanding lingers between individuals, strife results, which can lead to quarrelling and bitterness. We need to express godly love toward other human beings. Perhaps this may seem impossible at the beginning, but the more we practise, the easier it gets. "But whoso hath this world's good, and seeth his brother have need, and shutteth up his bowels of compassion from him, how dwelleth the love of God in him?" (1 John 3:17)

Perhaps we can learn from the apostle, Paul—a busy man of God in his day, yet he found time to relate with churches he founded and elders he appointed. In his reflections, he wrote that the greatest gift of all is *love*. According to him, other gifts may fail, but love never does. Biblical love is the most indispensible quality for the Christian.

> Though I speak with the tongues of men and of angels, and have not charity, I am become as sounding brass, or a tinkling cymbal. And though I have the gift of prophecy, and understand all mysteries, and all knowledge; and though I have all faith, so that I could remove mountains, and have not charity, I am nothing. And though I bestow all my goods to feed the poor, and though I give my body to be burned, and have not charity, it profiteth me nothing. Charity suffereth long, and is kind; charity envieth not; charity vaunteth not itself, is not puffed up, doth not behave itself unseemly, seeketh not her own, is not easily provoked, thinketh no evil; Rejoiceth not in iniquity, but rejoiceth in the truth; Beareth all things, believeth all things, hopeth all things, endureth all things. Charity never faileth: but whether there be prophecies, they shall fail; whether there be tongues, they shall cease; whether there be knowledge, it shall vanish away. For we

know in part, and we prophesy in part. But when that which is perfect is come, then that which is in part shall be done away. When I was a child, I spake as a child, I understood as a child, I thought as a child: but when I became a man, I put away childish things. For now we see through a glass, darkly; but then face to face: now I know in part; but then shall I know even as also I am known. And now abideth faith, hope, charity, these three; but the greatest of these is charity. (1 Corinthians 13:1–13)

Recently, I watched a documentary about a successful businessman in the United States of America. He owns a variety of business chains. He invests in failing businesses and turns them into outstanding investments. The amazing thing about this investor is that most of the time he has no knowledge of the inner workings of some of his businesses. This baffles many, so this documentary studied the secret of his success.

When his staff were interviewed, they spoke very well of him. They mentioned that their boss tells them in person that he appreciates them. He makes them feel valuable. He personally sends them cards for their birthdays and anniversaries. If he is on the premises for such days, he stops by their desks to wish them well. He also makes sure his staff knows he values their contribution to the company. He uses the same method for both junior and senior staff. One employee said, "After all he has done for us, how can I disrespect him or let him down?"

Though the man may be showing kindness primarily for the sake of his own profit, aspects of this attitude seem conspicuously like biblical love. We demonstrate love by being kind to others, not intimidating them. I have always thought that certain people sometimes confuse fear and respect. It is possible to fear someone and not respect them because of their demeaning or intimidating behaviour or character. When employees fear their employers, they may pretend to be working when the boss is around. However, a boss whose employees respect him does not have to be around for the staff to be productive. Maybe we could conclude by saying that love brings out the best in people, and it costs nothing but a simple and kind deed, word, or gesture.

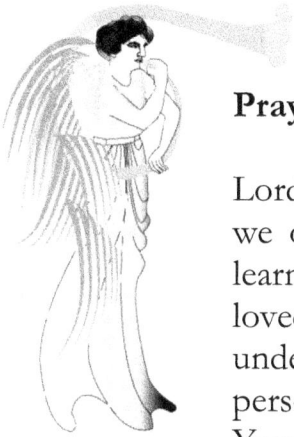

Prayer

Lord God Almighty, to You we offer our prayer. May we learn how to love as You have loved us. Help us to fully understand that You are love personified. You have said in Your Word that the person who does not love does not know You. Your Son commanded us to love one another as He has loved us. Heal the emotional wounds or stubbornness that causes us to ignore the teachings of Jesus Christ.

continued . . .

"Then came Peter to him, and said, Lord, how oft shall my brother sin against me, and I forgive him? till seven times? Jesus saith unto him, I say not unto thee, Until seven times: but, until seventy times seven" (Matt. 18:21–22). The Lord told us to forgive until seventy times seven. We know this is not easy, but we also know that it is not by might, nor by power, but by the help of the Holy Spirit that we can do so, in the name of Jesus Christ. "For if ye forgive men their trespasses, your heavenly Father will also forgive you" (Matt. 6:14).

In The Secret Place - Conversations With God

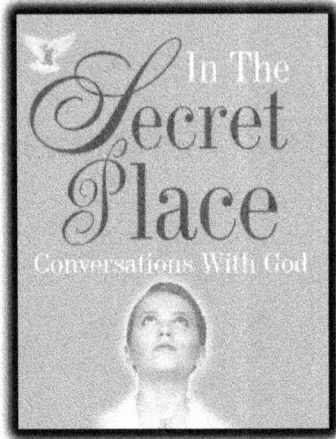

The atmosphere of worship enables us to express our devotion to God. While in it, the bruises we have incurred are getting healed without even having to utter a word to our Heavenly Father.

Chapter Seven

The Three Pillars

The three most powerful pillars that help in ushering the presence of the Lord into the Secret Place are gratitude, praise, and worship. King David set a good example of a person who was totally in love with God. He was obsessed with God and did not even allow his position as a king to change his attitude as a worshipper. He was passionate when it came to gratitude, praise, and worship. He was not concerned of his whereabouts when he needed to get into the 'worship zone'. A good example was discussed in chapter four when he danced in public, an act that offended his wife, Michal. He was not ashamed to acknowledge that his success as a powerful king was not of his own making but was a blessing from Almighty God. He was a ruthless warrior yet a humble man who knew when and how to lower himself in the presence of God.

Although David was a sinful person just like us, once he realized his mistakes, he never

75

wasted time in repenting. He collected himself and got on with the work ahead. In the Scripture below, David composed songs of gratitude to the Lord for his victories against the enemies. David's gratefulness seemed quite simple—not so different from a little child who is extremely excited and thankful to his earthly father because of receiving an unexpected gift. David praised God freely and was happy to thank Him. We should seek to be like David in the presence of God as we enter the Secret Place. We are thankful and are aware of His infinite greatness.

We know that God is aware of everything we have done or where we have been even before we begin to speak. And there is no mountain that He will not enable us to climb.

> And David spake unto the LORD the words of this song in the day that the LORD had delivered him out of the hand of all his enemies, and out of the hand of Saul: And he said, The LORD is my rock, and my fortress, and my deliverer; The God of my rock; in him will I trust: he is my shield, and the horn of my salvation, my high tower, and my refuge, my saviour; thou savest me from violence. I will call on the LORD, who

> is worthy to be praised: so shall I be saved from mine enemies. When the waves of death compassed me, the floods of ungodly men made me afraid; The sorrows of hell compassed me about; the snares of death prevented me; In my distress I called upon the LORD, and cried to my God: and he did hear my voice out of his temple, and my cry did enter into his ears. (2 Samuel 22: 1–7)

Abraham, too, was a worshipper and an intercessor. He was a man of God who was rewarded because of his unshaken faith in God. When he heard the voice of God, he didn't allow himself to be hurled into a state of 'reasoning himself into doubt'. "But when it pleased God, who separated me from my mother's womb, and called me by his grace to reveal his Son in me, that I might preach him among the heathen, immediately I conferred not with flesh and blood" (Gal. 1:15–16).

These words from the apostle Paul tell us that when he heard from God, he did not consult with flesh and blood; he trusted the voice of God.

Some of us are believing God to fulfil the promises we received through His Word. Others have prayed for many years and have not even seen a glimpse of hope. It now appears as though what's been asked for is never going to happen; however, it is not the time to lose hope. We have to stop consulting with flesh. We must hold on and keep praying while believing with full conviction that God is able!

Amazingly, in most cases the answers come packaged in layers of wrapping. We have to unwrap the package, which takes time, in order to get to the gift. What we prayed for is just in front of us, but we fail to accept it because it is not packaged as we had anticipated. We need to shut out all the voices and stop reasoning with the flesh so that we can clearly hear the voice of God. This is achieved only through worship and by separating ourselves from the crowd.

From time to time, the Lord withdrew from the crowds to spend time in the presence of God in prayer. It is important that we understand our need to sometimes pull away from others in order to hear from God. In the midst of many voices, when alone with God, we get revived and renewed. "And when he had sent the multitudes away, he went up into a mountain apart to pray; and when the evening was come, he was there alone" (Matt. 14:23).

When we are alone in the presence of God, we become complete. We are released from constant worry and anxiety, knowing that God is in control because we have allowed His will to be done in our lives. In this place we freely exercise the three pillars: thanksgiving (gratitude), praise, and worship. While I am in this Secret Place, I feel like dancing. I share my joy and my plans with the Lord. I am free here. This place is where dreams are birthed!

Have a pen and paper or a digital recorder ready so that you can write or record what the Holy Spirit reveals to you. The moment must be captured because it is not easy to recapture afterwards. When Moses went to Mount Sinai in the presence of the Almighty God, he was given two tables of stone. "And he gave unto Moses, when he had made an end of communing with him upon mount Sinai, two tables of testimony, tables of stone, written with the finger of God" (Ex. 31:18).

When we get into the presence of God a dialogue takes place. Moses was truly a great man of God who used his time in the presence of God to intercede for others. Again, he was able to repeat in detail to the Israelites conversations between him and God.

> And the LORD said unto Moses, I have seen this people, and, behold, it is a stiffnecked people: Now therefore let me alone, that my wrath may wax hot against them, and that I may consume them: and I will make of thee a great nation. And Moses besought the LORD his God, and said, LORD, why doth thy wrath wax hot against thy people, which thou hast brought forth out of the land of Egypt with great power, and with a mighty hand? Wherefore should the Egyptians speak, and say, For mischief did he bring them out, to slay them in the mountains, and to consume them from the face of the earth? Turn from thy fierce wrath, and repent of this evil against thy people. Remember Abraham, Isaac, and Israel, thy servants, to whom thou swearest by thine own self, and saidst unto them, I will multiply your seed as the stars of heaven, and all this land that I have spoken of will I give unto your seed, and they shall inherit it forever. And the LORD repented of the evil which he thought to do unto his people. (Exodus 32:9–14)

In Exodus 32, we see a picture of Moses as mediator and peacemaker. While Moses was talking to God, he was unaware that the Israelites had sinned. God was already aware of the Israelites' festival to the calf idol. He declared to His servant that the Israelites were a stiff-necked people whom He wanted to destroy. Yet Moses managed to convince God to turn from His anger and His planned action against the Israelites. Nevertheless, when Moses came down from Mount Sinai and act saw what the people had done, he was furious. He crashed to pieces the stone tables on which God had written the Ten Commandments. In the later verses, we see Moses going back to God to inform Him that the Israelites had committed a great sin. He does not stop at that; Moses beseeches God to forgive the Israelites. Presumably, he felt in some sense responsible because he asked God to blot him out of His book.

> And Moses returned unto the LORD, and said, Oh, this people have sinned a great sin, and have made them gods of gold. Yet now, if thou wilt forgive their sin—; and if not, blot me, I pray thee, out of thy book which thou hast written. And the LORD said unto Moses, Whosoever hath sinned against me, him will I blot out of my book. Therefore now go, lead the people unto the place of which I have spoken unto thee: behold, mine Angel shall go before thee: nevertheless in the day when I visit, I will visit their sin upon them. And the LORD

> plagued the people, because they made the
> calf, which Aaron made. (Exodus 32:31–35)

Moses demonstrated an act of love of a selfless leader, an intercessor, and a peacemaker. We can learn a lot from Moses that could contribute to a fruitful fellowship with our Maker. Despite the high position as a friend of God and a man who talked with God, Moses was humble. He demonstrated the godly character as manifested by God in all the attributes of emotions that we, too, possess. Moses was becoming more and more like God in character.

God authorized Moses to speak to Pharaoh as though God Himself stood before the Egyptian leader. This is as stated in the Scripture, God said to Moses to tell the Israelites that He had sent Moses to them. "And God said unto Moses, I AM THAT I AM: and he said, Thus shalt thou say unto the children of Israel, I AM hath sent me unto you" (Ex. 3:14). Moses was a mediator, that is, an intermediary between God and His people.

If we do what is necessary to create the needed environment in the Secret Place, we are able to converse with God just as Moses did.

Had the Israelites listened to their leader and obeyed the Word of the Lord, some of them would not have perished in the wilderness. They were assured that there was no need to fear the enemy because God was with them. In spite of that, their minds were already corrupted with doubt, fear, and bitterness (Num. 14:14).

Moses' humility is portrayed through his action as a mediator—in the ways he handled the complicated state of affairs that concerned the Israelites. At no point do we read in the Scripture that Moses berated the Israelites, declaring that God wanted to kill them because of their rebellious nature, and boasting that he interceded for them (see v. 12). The humble Moses had the Word of the Lord and a promised covenant to Abraham's seed by God. "And God said unto Abraham, Thou shalt keep my covenant therefore, thou, and thy seed after thee in their generations" (Gen. 17:9). God was looking for a people whom He would fill with His glory, a people who would not reject His call to go up to Him.

Despite the people's troublesome nature, Moses sent out ten spies to traverse the Promised Land. They brought back fruits, such as the pomegranates, figs, and grapes. Despite all the goodness they saw of in the land, all but two of the spies convinced themselves and the people that it was impossible to enter Canaan because were giants were there. They trashed all the promises God had given them concerning the land.

In the Secret Place we may gain a vision or a taste of the glory of God, but it is how we conduct ourselves afterwards that demonstrates any true spiritual breakthrough. The Israelites saw themselves as unlikely candidates for the Promised Land. Earlier, they had seen the glory of God leading them day and night out of the wilderness, yet as the breakthrough was nearing, they lost faith and hope. Two of the spies, Caleb and Joshua, had a conquering spirit: They believed God unquestioningly. Many enter the presence of God and receive revelatory promises but then fail to manifest these promises because of their disbelief (see Num. 13:23–33).

God invited them, but they chose rather to listen to men. If God felt they were not ready, He would not have asked them to meet with Him. Likewise, God has given us an open invitation to meet with Him, but often we have chosen to worship or heed humans in the place of God. We have ignored the need to fellowship with God, even though this process has now been simplified for us. Christ gave up His life on the cross as a ransom for our sin. He broke down the wall of partition between humanity and God; we now have direct access into the presence of God because our righteousness is in Christ.

We need to listen to what God has to say to each of us individually as well as corporately—and that takes time. We have to get to that point where we can identify our connection with Abba, Father.

Our lives will be much better for it. Doing so will protect us from being swayed by hearsay. Let us go to the Secret Place where the Lord will teach us His ways. When we are born again, our Mount Zion is in us through the sweet Spirit of our God.

Jesus Christ said that the kingdom of God is in us and around us. We become citizens of heaven, of which Christ is the Head. He who is joined with the Lord is one Spirit with Him.

Moses stood in the presence of the Lord for forty days and forty nights without eating or drinking. When he came out he had to cover his face with a veil because his face was too bright for the Israelites to behold. They couldn't look at him. "And when Aaron and all the children of Israel saw Moses, behold, the skin of his face shone; and they were afraid to come nigh him" (Ex. 34:30).

God is yearning for a glory nation—a New Jerusalem, where people will run to worship almighty Jesus, the Light of the World. They will hurry into God's presence to feel His touch.

It's true that darkness disappears when the light shows up. Christ declared that believers are the light of the world. We can change difficult surroundings in our 'world' if we stay close to the bright shining star. Christ is the star of David, who called us out of darkness into His marvelous light. Jesus said He is the Light of the World; therefore, whoever stays close to Him shall overcome the world. In the Secret Place under the shadow of the Almighty, we receive power to tear down strongholds.

When the light shines on us, our vision becomes clear. Every crooked path is set straight. Worshiping God and having the knowledge of His Presence can be achieved in the Secret Place. As Moses went up on Mount Sinai to be with the Lord God, he took Joshua with him. Christ went up a high mountain and took with Him Peter, James, and John and was transfigured before them. It is written that his face did shine as the sun, and his raiment was white as the light. "And after six days Jesus taketh Peter, James, and John his brother, and bringeth them up into an high mountain apart, and was transfigured before them: and his face did shine as the sun, and his raiment was white as the light. And, behold, there appeared unto them Moses and Elias talking with him" (Matt. 17:1–3).

Peter, James, John, and Andrew went to the Lord privately to enquire regarding things they did not understand (Mark 13:3). When Moses heard the call from God, he dedicated his whole self to the work of God. In turn, he was fortunate to converse with God as a friend.

Due to their commitment to the Lord, the disciples were warranted privileges that granted them access to the secrets of the kingdom. "The secret of the LORD is with them that fear him; and he will shew them his covenant" (Ps. 25:14). Jesus of Nazareth made time to be alone with His Father. "And when it was day, he departed and went into a desert place: and the people sought him, and came unto him, and stayed him, that he should not depart from them" (Luke 4:42).

Worshipping the Lord opens doors that we never imagined possible. It is, therefore, crucial for us to understand the importance of the pillar of worship as we prepare ourselves to get into the Secret Place of the Most High God under His shadow. This is where we are privileged to experience God's love, where we are reborn while we are simultaneously surrounded with God's love. His kindness embraces us.

Prayer

Oh, Lord God, thou art God who reigns above the earth. Teach us how to worship as You have purposed. Teach us new songs, new sounds. Give us supernatural voices that can connect with the angels in heaven as they worship You. Show us how to use instruments as David did—the tambourine, saxophone, organ, trumpet, drums, guitar, and flute—accompanied with unique tunes as we join the angels in heaven singing:

continued . . .

"And hast made us unto our God kings and priests: and we shall reign on the earth. And I beheld, and I heard the voice of many angels round about the throne and the beasts and the elders: and the number of them was ten thousand times ten thousand, and thousands of thousands; Saying with a loud voice, Worthy is the Lamb that was slain to receive power, and riches, and wisdom, and strength, and honour, and glory, and blessing. And every creature which is in heaven, and on the earth, and under the earth, and such as are in the sea, and all that are in them, heard I saying: *Blessing, and honour, and glory, and power, be unto him that sitteth upon the throne, and unto the Lamb forever and ever. And the four beasts said, Amen. And the four and twenty elders fell down and worshipped him that liveth forever and ever*" (Rev. 5:10–14). Amen.

Chapter Eight

The Glory of the Lord

When the glory of the Lord fills the temple, we are assured that God is with us and our prayers have been heard. At this point through Christ, we are able to boldly converse with the Almighty, as Abraham and Moses did.

A certain height exists in the spiritual realm, which, perhaps, few believers enjoy. When I say this, I do not mean that it is achievable only for a few 'super spiritual' saints; however, I believe it is true that our daily lifestyles does determine, to some extent, our level of intimacy with Him. Our relationships with those around us, whether at home, at work, or wherever we are, if not pleasing to God could cost us our highest destiny. If we do not love those around us with an unconditional love, it is impossible to love God, whom we have not seen. God is pure! He is Holy! The angel declared, Holy is the Lord God Almighty; heaven and earth are filled with

His Glory. Hosanna to the Highest. "The Lord is high above all nations, and his glory above the heavens" (Ps. 113:4).

My desire is that this revelation will help all of us understand how important it is to lead a life of holiness. It is impossible to gauge what we may have missed as Christians because we have failed to maintain a godly standard. The Holy Spirit is sent to help and empower us. It is not by human might, nor by power, but by the Holy Spirit that God's things are accomplished. The Holy Spirit is rarely acknowledged in some circles. On very few occasions do we come across a fellow believer who is full to overflowing with the Holy Spirit, yet He is the most important person in a believer's life. If welcomed, the Holy Spirit prompts us to glorify the Lord, to help us rectify the evil that takes place in our lives, and to enable us to receive the benefits that come with it. When the glory fills the temple, everything becomes new. The privilege of being in the glory of the Lord enables us to intercede and call things into being.

> And Moses said unto the LORD, See, thou sayest unto me, Bring up this people: and thou hast not let me know whom thou wilt send with me. Yet thou hast said, I know

thee by name, and thou hast also found grace in my sight. Now therefore, I pray thee, if I have found grace in thy sight, shew me now thy way, that I may know thee, that I may find grace in thy sight: and consider that this nation is thy people. And he said, My presence shall go with thee, and I will give thee rest. And he said unto him, If thy presence go not with me, carry us not up hence. For wherein shall it be known here that I and thy people have found grace in thy sight? is it not in that thou goest with us? so shall we be separated, I and thy people, from all the people that are upon the face of the earth. And the LORD said unto Moses, I will do this thing also that thou hast spoken: for thou hast found grace in my sight, and I know thee by name. And he said, I beseech thee, shew me thy glory. And he said, I will make all my goodness pass before thee, and I will proclaim the name of the LORD before thee; and will be gracious to whom I will be gracious, and will shew mercy on whom I will shew mercy. And he said, Thou canst not see my face: for there shall no man see me, and live. And the LORD said, Behold, there is a place by me, and thou shalt stand upon a rock: And it shall come to pass, while my glory passeth by, that I will put thee in a cleft of the rock, and will cover thee with my hand while I pass by: And I will take away mine hand, and thou shalt see my back parts: but my face shall not be seen. (Exodus 33:12–23)

While in the spiritual atmosphere, we can receive an impartation to godly creativity. New ideas are released! On the other hand, our attitudes and grumblings can shut down the manifestation of God's glory. While in the desert, the Israelites thought they were murmuring against Moses and Aaron, unaware it was God against whom they rebelled (Ex. 16:5–15). Moses informed them that their complaining was against God. We learn then that when we complain against those God has chosen, we are actually placing ourselves in opposition to God Himself. The best we can and should do is intercede for them, to allow God's perfect will to overrule in any situation. Those who took part in the murmuring did not get to the Promised Land (Num. 14:16–26).

The overwhelming splendour and greatness of God's glory abound in us if only we learn the secret of maintaining a godly atmosphere. The Scripture states that when the glory of the Lord came down upon Mt. Sinai, the cloud covered it for six days. "And the glory of the LORD abode upon mount Sinai, and the cloud covered it six days: and the seventh day he called unto Moses out of the midst of the cloud. And the sight of the glory of the LORD was like devouring fire on the top of the mount in the eyes of the children of Israel" (Ex. 24:16–17). In some cases the glory of the Lord will abide for days until the intended purpose is achieved.

The angels declared, "Glory to God in the highest, and on earth peace, good will toward men" (Luke 2:14). As we glorify God, our lives are renewed! He, in turn, makes known to us the riches of his glory.

And that he might make known the riches of his glory on the vessels of mercy, which he had afore prepared unto glory, even us, whom he hath called, not of the Jews only, but also of the Gentiles? As he saith also in Osee, I will call them my people, which were not my people; and her beloved, which was not beloved. And it shall come to pass, that in the place where it was said unto them, Ye are not my people; there shall they be called the children of the living God. (Romans 9:23–26)

God forbids us to share His glory with anyone or anything. When things that were declared beforehand according to His Word come to pass, it magnifies His character to the peoples. He reveals new things beforehand so that we may glorify Him. Truly, His Word is settled in heaven. He is not a man that He should lie (Num. 23:9). It is therefore an abomination when some of us say that God has spoken to us to do certain things or to be some place and are adamant that we have heard from God. Then when our fleshly goals are not fulfilled, we quickly backtrack, thinking up some new message God 'has given' to explain our inaccurate prophecies. Our credibility becomes increasingly questionable when we recklessly claim we have a direct Word from God yet it is not manifested. Could we possibly mistake our fleshly desire for a Word from God?

God could assign a person to a specific task and trust them to carry on with it. When obedience is fulfilled but the people did not receive the messenger, God through His Holy Spirit would send the person to a different location to deliver His message. We will be judged on the last day for the misuse of the Holy Spirit and for using God's name in a vain manner. We must be very careful. "And whosoever speaketh a word against the Son of man, it shall be forgiven him: but whosoever speaketh against the Holy Ghost, it shall not be forgiven him, neither in this world, neither in the world to come" (Matt. 12:32).

Jesus instructed His disciples to go to a town to preach the gospel. "And whosoever shall not receive you, nor hear your words, when ye depart out of that house or city, shake off the dust of your feet" (Matt. 10:14). He asked them to leave the town if they were not welcomed. However I am a little puzzled by the many of us who claim we have a Word from the Holy Spirit for hostile unbelievers, when we should actually be 'shaking the dust' off our feet. We need to read the Bible and understand who the Holy Spirit is and what His assignment is to us.

The most powerful thing in the whole world is the WORD of God. As the glory of the Lord is revealed to us, loneliness is overcome with joy. We receive strength and become confident to preach or do the tasks that have been waiting for a long time.

Some do glory in darkness rather than exalting the name of Jesus Christ; such are best eradicated from our fellowship. The false doctrine maligning the Word of God mixes truth with the traditions of men. These doctrines threaten to devour the saints of God. Even the elect, if not careful, could be deceived. I pray for mercy on us. These are the times to stay alert and pray without ceasing. Those who guard their loins with the Word of God shall overcome.

Rather than glorying in being glorified, we should get into the Secret Place and converse with God for His will and purpose to be manifest and that evil would be vanquished. It's unfortunate that we want to be acknowledged in every little thing we do for God. Even as attendees or members of a ministry or congregation, we sometimes run after special attention and praise. Some unwisely claim that God has called them to be in a prominent position in a church or ministry. They go with the hidden motive of finding a quick way to climb the ladder of leadership and authority. In so doing, they are disappointed when ambitions are not welcomed in those places.

We must learn to obey and learn to hear from God where He wants us to be at any particular time or with whom we are assigned. Then we would never be disappointed, and God alone would get the glory. David said he would rather be a gatekeeper in the house of the Lord: "For a day in thy courts is better than a thousand. I had rather be a doorkeeper in the house of my God, than to dwell in the tents of wickedness" (Ps. 84:10). If we surrender ourselves completely to God and let Him be in charge, every stumbling block in our paths will be removed out of the way. Peace will be within us. When we are in the right place at the right time and are submissive to those in authority, grace will abound and strife will not be a part of us. This will bring glory to the Lord's name.

When we allow the Lord to work through us, we do not need to constantly prove ourselves to those around us that God is at work through us. Everything becomes obvious at the appointed time. We must serve God wholeheartedly without murmuring, even when no one sees us, knowing that the Lord does. This will cause God to glorify Himself in us and through us.

He will reward you publicly because you're not after the approval of men but of the almighty God! When you tell your loved ones you love them, they sometimes will reply that they love you too. When in your Secret Place conversing with God, when you express your love for Him and to Him, do not be surprised if, unexpectedly, God sends someone to let you know how much He loves you. In the New Testament, the apostle Peter is acknowledged by the mighty anointing that was upon him so that even his shadow healed the sick. Is it any wonder? Peter met a lame man sitting at the gate of the temple, asking for alms. Peter realized the man needed more than money. Instead of providing him what he requested, Peter commanded the man to rise up and walk in the name of Jesus Christ of Nazareth)Acts 3:1–8).

Disciples were careful not to interfere with God's glory. They understood they were chosen by grace as vessels to serve God. They were moved by the Holy Spirit.

> And when Silas and Timotheus were come from Macedonia, Paul was pressed in the spirit, and testified to the Jews that Jesus was Christ. And when they opposed themselves, and blasphemed, he shook his raiment, and said unto them, Your blood be upon your own heads; I am clean: from henceforth I will go unto the Gentiles. And he departed thence, and entered into a certain man's house, named Justus, one that worshipped God, whose house joined hard

> to the synagogue. And Crispus, the chief ruler of the synagogue, believed on the Lord with all his house; and many of the Corinthians hearing believed, and were baptized. Then spake the Lord to Paul in the night by a vision, Be not afraid, but speak, and hold not thy peace: For I am with thee, and no man shall set on thee to hurt thee: for I have much people in this city. (Acts 18:5–10)

God is able to minister through you to an individual from whom nobody expects anything good. Who knows whether, in turn, God will then use that person to shake the nations and make history if we touch not His glory? It is good when one is acknowledged for what God is doing, but it should be in a manner that glorifies God.

Eli and his sons were serving God when Samuel came to join them; however, this family fell out of the glory of God because of sin. Their action resulted in the glory of God departing from Israel in their season. Yet because Samuel was faithful toward God, he didn't take part in their sinful life. God anointed him mightily in the decades to follow as one of the greatest of Israel's prophets.

> He will keep the feet of his saints, and the

wicked shall be silent in darkness; for by strength shall no man prevail. The adversaries of the LORD shall be broken to pieces; out of heaven shall he thunder upon them: the LORD shall judge the ends of the earth; and he shall give strength unto his king, and exalt the horn of his anointed. And Elkanah went to Ramah to his house. And the child did minister unto the LORD before Eli the priest. (1 Samuel 2:9–11)

Now the sons of Eli were sons of Belial; they knew not the LORD. (1 Samuel 2:12)

To some the glory has departed long ago. *Ichabod* could well be written over their lives. They are aware but continue to deceive others. Even so, as in Samuel's case, God has appointed someone else to carry on in their places. All from whom the glory has departed speak of what God did through them long ago. They don't acknowledge that they have been laid aside and replaced. There is no new thing God is doing through them. Sadly, the glory has departed because of their sinful lives. It is difficult to recapture lost glory. "And she named the child Ichabod, saying, The glory is departed from Israel: because the ark of God was taken, and because of her father in law and her husband. And she said, The glory is departed from Israel: for the ark of God is taken" (1 Sam. 4:21–22).

We are created to worship and glorify God, and we must lift up the name of Jesus Christ in all that we do. The name of Jesus Christ is above every other name. "Who hath saved us, and called us with an holy calling, not according to our works, but according to his own purpose and grace, which was given us in Christ Jesus before the world began" (2 Tim. 1:9).

Prayer

Heavenly Father, help us understand how important it is to worship You and that You do not share Your glory with any other. Deliver us from fear of the unknown, and lead us to the place where we will be safe. "Fear ye not, neither be afraid: have not I told thee from that time, and have declared it? ye are even my witnesses. Is there a God beside me? yea, there is no God; I know not any" (Isa. 44:8). Thank You for hearing our prayer in Jesus' mighty name. Amen.

Testimony

Here's a recent Testimony from a reader in London, UK: "Hi Priscar, I am glad I got in touch with you. When you prayed, God spoke through you to me all the things that have been in my heart this morning. I believed God to secure our business further, and to establish it. God also confirmed to me through you the same messages that a great prophet from USA also told me. Thank you very much, and may God continue to bless you and your Ministry!

Bro. D. Clarke, London, UK

About the Author

Priscar Manei is an anointed prophetic evangelist with a great passion to see souls come to Christ. She was raised in a good Christian home and was dedicated to the path of a ministerial call. The Lord has been preparing her for ministry under the mentorship of several great pastors and leaders. She has served a total of seven years in various capacities, including leading intercession in prayer meetings. She is the author of *Surviving the Wilderness: On the Way to Your Destiny*, which highlights the significance of servitude and how each of us has a part to play.

www.Priscar4Jesus.Com
E-mail: Priscar4Jesus@gmail.com

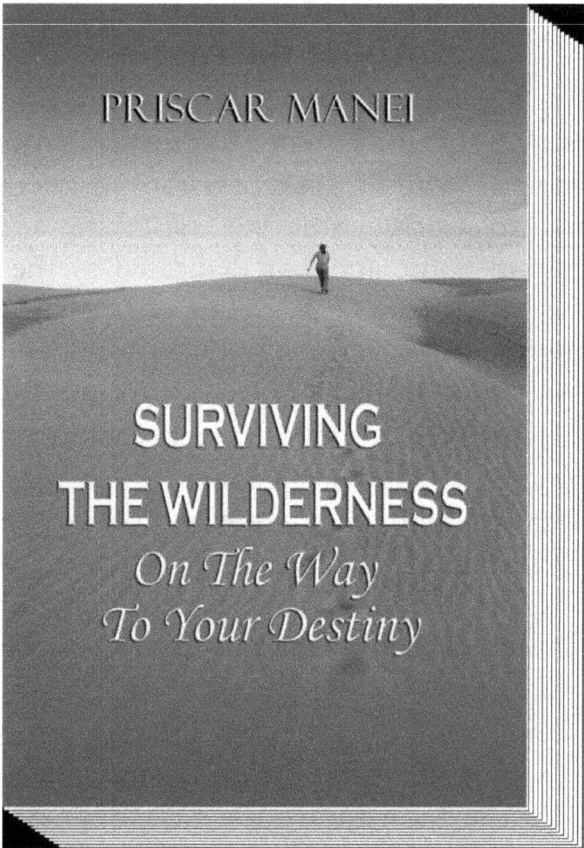

PRISCAR MANEI

SURVIVING
THE WILDERNESS
On The Way
To Your Destiny

Please order your copy today!

Hello New Friend & Reader of *In the Secret Place* ...

Please drop me a line to let me know how this book is helping you, especially if the messages and revelations within it have triggered something new in you to make you run to get even closer to God! Send me your testimony, and please also feel free to include any prayer requests you may have.

I'll be glad to pray for you! E-mail me at: Priscar4Jesus@gmail.com. Thanks!

The secret of the LORD is with them that fear him; and he will shew them his covenant.

Psalm 25:14

And I will give thee the treasures of darkness, and hidden riches of secret places, that thou mayest know that I, the LORD, which call thee by thy name, am the God of Israel.

Isaiah 45:3

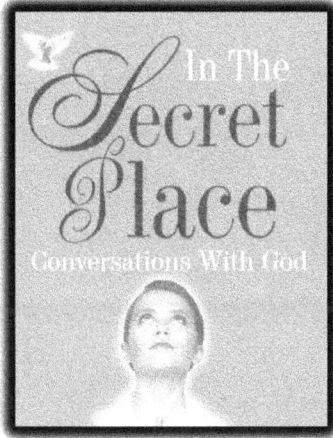

*All things are possible with God
to those who believe.*

Glory to God in
the highest,
and on earth
peace, good will
toward men.

Luke 2:14